IRIS' EYES
poetry for the mind, heart and soul

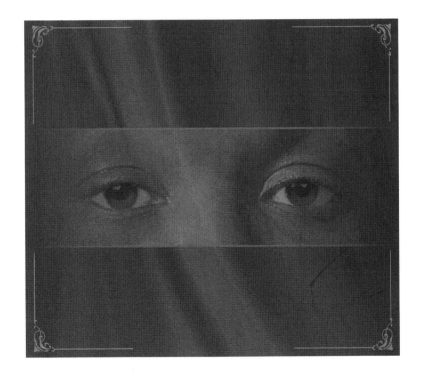

Patrice Iris Smith

IRIS' EYES | poetry for the mind, heart and soul

ISBN-10: 154075913X
ISBN-13: 978-1540759139
Copyright © 2016 by Patrice Smith
All rights reserved.

Printed by CreateSpace, an Amazon.com company.
www.CreateSpace.com
Available from Amazon.com and other retail outlets.

www.facebook.com/patricesbooks/

Contents

Dedication 5
Foreword 7
Prelude 9

IMPRESSIONS 12
Estrella (Star) Brilliance 12
A Vintage Treasure 12
Boy in the Band 13
Mystical Magic 14
Vantage Point 15
B-A-B-Y 16
Ambivalence Claim 17
Humanity in Motion 19
Blended Blues of Euphoria 20
Lunar Mysteries 21
Like a Whispering Wind 22
Deep Down Transition 22
A Squared Configuration 23
Rendezvous at the Shore 24
Lasting Imprint 25

EXPRESSIONS 27
Admiration 28
Tribute to Fathers 29
A Modest Prayer for the New Generation 30
The Gift 31
Regret Full 32
Looking Outward 33

What Resonates in Your Soul? 34
Unruly Crown 35
The Heart of the Soul 36
A to F Sharp# 36
De-Selection 37
First Place Losers 38
Interlocked 38
Slippers 39
An Angel's Touch 39
Jack-y 40
Take the Ride 40
Burst of Purple 41
Shared Day by Birth 41
Up Right Down 42
A Right to Be Free 43
Remembering JE 44
Sunset's Solace 44
Mind Detox 45
Speak On It! 46
True Sisters 47
This Special Day 47
Whisper of the Voiceless 48

REFLECTIONS 49
Saturn's Mystical Unveiling 50
The Day Before 51
Restful Moments 52
Our "Oui" (We) Time 52

The Task of Time 53
Warm Expectation 54
Journey 55
Stolen (by Alzheimer's Disease) 56
His Rod and Staff 57
3:17 am 57
Real Truths 58
Tears Unleashed 58
If / Then 59
Enlightened Awakening 59
The Sparrow and Me 60
No One Quite Like You 61
Giving Plentiful Thanks 61
Iris' Eyes 62
Mood Masters 63
Guitar Bandit 64
Twelve Empty Vases 65

REVELATIONS 67
Hazy Perceptions 68
What If 69
Simply Complex 70
2 ° Below 71
Let Silence Ring 72
Nature's Best 73
The Path Unpaved 75

DEDICATION

In Loving Memory

In loving memory of my mother, Grace, my greatest inspiration.
My "Admiration" for you will forever remain in my heart..

In Memory of My Mother
How can I say I remember
her smile that was wistfully gay
How can I ever tell you
about her understanding way
How can words express
her constant and tender care
How can I make you feel
the depth of her despair
I can only tell you I loved her

Author – Grace E. Lester
Submitted by your daughter Patrice

For my children and grandchildren, the pulsations of my life
Toni, Jamal, Brandi, Ricardo, Jonathan, and Jackson

FOREWORD

A Vision from Iris' Eyes

Someone said that, "Nothing comes to a dreamer but a dream" and this may be true, but only if the vision ends there. Why can't it be that we begin our wondrous journey with the sparkling tiny fragments of the mind's imagination? That is exactly what I set out to do in my first book of poems. I wanted to bring my simple yet intricate thoughts and feelings into the realm of light and thrust them to the surface by syncing them to paper with the written word. These ideas will always be somewhat of a work in progress because my thoughts are forever flowing and interlocking with new ones on the verge of topics to explore. The fusion of my physical and creative energy first fueled me to record my thoughts and express myself decades ago. But like many budding writers, for much of this time, I've found myself caught in a "yo-yo" writing pattern. Since I decided to take the plunge and publish, I've had many periods inspiration to write only to be abruptly faced with extended times of writer's block when nothing would formulate and take shape. It is at these times that I usually abstain from writing altogether but always continue to engage in conscious conversation with my mind garnering new ideas. It has taken many bits and pieces gathered together from time to time over recent years to get here. I've nurtured this assortment of ideas while experimenting with various composition forms and style. I believe that the mind must first become saturated with thought before seeking a way to bring it together. What seemingly can begin as only an inkling of thought from a fanciful dream could possibly one day become an inspiration for someone when read from a page. Now that my poetry project has come full circle I hope that my voice will be heard throughout the pages of this book.

This book is divided into 4 sections - **Reflections, Impressions, Expressions,** and **Revelations**. It is written in a blend of poetic prose and rhythmic spoken word. Most of the content is rooted in and extracted from the many experiences that have impacted my life in some way. Others reflect hopes and dreams of ideals. Finally, there are poems inspired from ordinary people, i.e., family members, friends, and even strangers who have crossed my path and somehow touched my heart or shaped my thinking, therefore leaving me with a desire to write. This is the poetry of the mind's heart and soul embodied in the spirit of a personal collection of words.

I would be regretful if I did not acknowledge those who paved a way that helped me along on this wonderful journey. It has indeed come from very humble beginnings and sometimes meandered aimlessly along the way. I want to foremost acknowledge my dear friend, teacher, storyteller and writer, Carolyn Alex, my soul inspirer. Thanks for your encouragement and persistent urges to "take the leap", and then not to stop but take another. I did it because you believed I could and you simply would not let me allow the flame to burn down and go out. Thanks also to Cherryl W, posthumously for first submitting a few of my poems to our sorority's organization for publishing and provided a platform for my first audience. That simple action gave me confidence and helped me realize that I needed to move forward. I was further inspired by friend and English teacher, Natalie S. whose knowledge and expertise I highly regard. As I watched you instruct in the classroom, it helped me better understand the "feeling" of poetry and then providing guidance in structuring it to maximize its impact on the reader. I consider it a privilege to have worked with you professionally having gained invaluable knowledge about the magic of the written word. No one can give life to a Nikki Giovanni poem like you! To Belinda F, my dear friend who taught English for many years to students in very engaging and enjoyable ways. Because of you, they developed a love for literature and drama. In many of their eyes, I saw a passionate desire to dig deeper to learn more. I really appreciate you taking the time to carefully review my work, help me organize it and offer invaluable feedback. I took every word, idea, and suggestion to heart as I progressed. Thanks to Charissa J, for your professional editing skills and comments. I gained some valuable information from you. To my daughter, Toni, I can't thank you enough for your wealth of knowledge and computer skills. Your hands-on approach in putting the pieces together, from beginning to end is so appreciated. I'm forever indebted to you! By no means, would this book be in existence now without the work, of Larry S., a graphic designer and author, who listened to my desires and simply got it done with proficient expertise. I appreciate your time, suggestions, and most of all your patience in helping me to do it right and get it done. An author always needs a friend who has an anytime willing ear to be there to listen, and lend encouragement, even when your ideas are sometimes quirky and unconventional. Carolyn A., you were that person for me! You literally "walked with me" through the last part of this long journey and patiently endured my random thoughts and countless claims that "I've got a poem for that!", as we strolled along during our fitness walks. Finally, I thank all unnamed friends and others who were there to support my effort in some way, even if just to give a casual smile or nudge of encouragement. I've always felt the inspiration to keep striving to reach my goal because I thought it would somehow be worth it in the end… and I can truly say, "Yes", it has been! Many Thanks!

Patrice Iris Smith

PRELUDE TO A POEM

Before a word appeared etched in sensory ink

from a divine inspiration, that formulated a link

Preceded by a thought of something uniquely unnamed

A phenomenal expression sparked an undeniable impression

Rendering an idea birthed from the cerebral depths of mind

Even ahead of its inception, a burning interjection silently emerged

biding time deep down in the pit of a restless searching soul

Its debut in birth speaks volumes, now eagerly consuming the

pages of blank spaces in a book

IMPRESSIONS

Estrella (Star) Brilliance

A star can never be denied her true luster and shine
To illuminate and lead the way is her only calling
She shatters utter darkness with a persistent unshakable force
It's no wonder she has been so perfectly purposed by the heavens
and placed on this phenomenal journey of generosity
just to shed her radiant light before our blinded eyes
She mystically attracts and captures our magnetic attention
Her light, unrestrained, spellbinding, nothing withheld, radiates throughout
No secret corners or angled bends can deny the path it knows it must travel
because that's the mission and her light will inevitably prevail for the world
to see and follow

A Vintage Treasure

Austere beauty glistens in her silver streaked hair
Casting splints of shimmering lights that reflect her
insight and wisdom of many years of favor
Faintly seen rings lie deep in her coffee brown eyes
A close look and quickly one thing you're sure of
She's "got it" and you want to know more about it
Her aged beauty fiercely rises in your presence urging you to
open the door, come up close to the stage, and see her performance

Boy in the Band

Surrendering to the band means
I can *finally* give the drummer some
of that pulsating rhythm from my mellow mood
He's here now moving rhythmically in sync with me
capturing my totally undivided attention
focusing my mind on the magic of the moment
that will never be repeated by any kind of replication
So I sit here entranced in my own self-indulgence
listening to the beat of the sound of his magnificent sticks
as they rap, tap, tap against my heart and draw me closer
I feel his tempo and it moves my hands and feet to his beat
sending me rocking into a back and forth then sideways groove
I'm rapidly swept away by these escalating moments
that are causing a steady increase in my now rising pulse
Alas! my true prince has finally come to rescue me
entwining me in a joyful ecstasy
bringing with him the possibility,
that it will envelop me in such sheer totality
sure to trigger a release of my suppressed energy
which for so long has been lingering in my soul
Oh yes, now I'm sure I know
that my heart beats solely for the man
with the wooden sticks dancing in his hands!

IRIS' EYES | poetry for the mind, heart and soul

Mystical Magic

One day at a slight glance,
I first noticed her picture-perfect lips
so faultlessly shaped from top to tip
They were precisely and carefully sectioned
like brightly cool tangerine slices in the sunlight
I marveled at how they glistened so radiantly
at the fixed objects that reflected upon them
In the flashing moment of flickering speckled light
I became aware that they blended so naturally in the
warm shadow of her caramel-colored complexion
and soft oval face that I never noticed before now

The next time I saw them, they were pursed horizontally
facing slightly away from view, positioned at the point where beginning
succinctly meets the corners of a rounded end and occupying a
place where they would be captured in the eye of a camera that day
while resting under the glowing rays of the beaming artificial light
where memories would be made

When angled just right, they held a mysterious revealing charm
that with a simple push of a button on the device that precisely
captured an unforgettable moment leaving a pleasant memory
In an instant, the innocence of their beauty did indeed define her
making a claim that represented an "oh so" perfect moment
"Click, click" the photo shoot was quickly over and the magic moment
 vanished

Now they will appear covered in hues of blazing orange or stunning pinks
as they are flawlessly postured on the page for a lipstick ad in a chic magazine
This will surely catch someone's attention tomorrow as they flip through the pages
of the beauty section looking for products to buy that will replenish their vitality

Vantage Point

Cotton soft snow arrived one cold winter morn and everything stood still

No sounds or echoes could be heard from earth's firmament or ground

It changed the landscape and suddenly there was no more visible barren land

Poised by the edge of a windowsill, became an ideal place, a vantage point

to think or to read or begin to write

to watch the movement of a special tree,

to observe a change, a covering of the old, the birth of a new

and natural wonders yet to be

So tranquil and fixed, it lay with no disruption to its pure and natural form

nothing changed and time purposely continued to carry on

until the unexpected arrival of a robin one unkind windy morn

bringing renewed hope for a brighter day

warmly chirping a new song, a welcome now to a longing fulfilled

a respite at last, from the winter's long spell

ushering in a sign of something soon to be

the return of spring and a new awakening

B-A-B-Y

He's brand new

We met him just now

Yet I'm sure we've known him before

His meaningful look and deep thoughtful eyes

There is something inside that we can't seem to define

We see a look so familiar as we watch from our side

This is our gift, a tiny baby boy, a genuine bundle of joy

His first day here, we've waited anxiously for him to arrive

and are now discovering a unique personality already forming

determined to be who he is, despite our imagined predictions

It's quickly taking shape and form while drawing our attention

in his direction, so that we will have no thoughts of doubt of who he is

He'll be carrying a family namesake, making our hearts overjoyed

Could it be possible that maybe we're only just meeting him

for the very first time or have we met him somewhere at a time before?

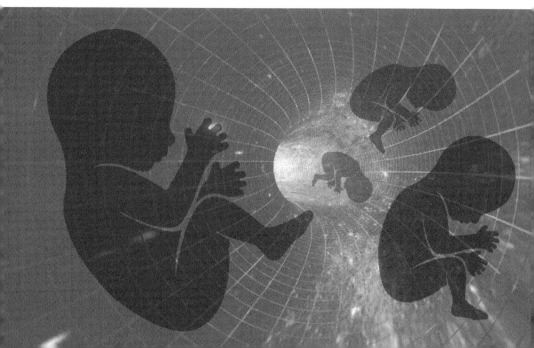

Ambivalence Claim

In the midst of trying to make a precise decision
existent thoughts and feelings often arise only to
clash and conflict
Thrashing in contradiction against the walls of
choosing a solution that perfectly fits
Eventually signs will arise that problems exist
at the intersect of what to do or not to do
Will it be that or this?
Looking aside from the fact, it might be a time
to take a calculated risk
The foe forces can be triggered to reach
increasing levels of doubt which steadily
sway the pendulum from side to side
while creating a back and forth pattern
of indecisiveness

        When the door of opportunity opens
        a choice must be made but somehow
        absolute certainty never seems to arrive
        sometimes, advancing forward, but then
        doubling back instead to find its way out
        of the confusion created by
        persistent tinges of doubt
        In the midst of it all and encircled by
        perfect uncertainty, the mind wretchedly
        wrangles with the choices it must make

Ambivalent thoughts and feelings running amok
clashing at the crossroads of taking a stand
to say *yes or no* and simply walk way
They follow a directionless path that stop to
contemplate briefly at the intersection of maybe so
A well-grounded force then backs away from
the need to commit and make its mark at all
to choose the path of what's more desired now
becomes something impossible to understand

        Now the final steps become more difficult to take
        even while standing at the threshold of something great
        With no way to know about which way to go
        Reaching a precise decision now has finally come face to face
        with its inevitable fate and all of the pieces quickly crumble
        All that's left to wonder is will there ever be another chance
        to consider the options without contradiction of thought
        If given another chance, simply choose what seems to be the
        right thing to do

Humanity in Motion

Wake up to be thankful for a new day to see
Look up to get up and gear up to go out and be
Free to make choices to do with it or without
Leaving behind the so warmly familiar for awhile
in exchange for an experience of some doubt *then*
Set out, to take action, prepared to keep things balanced and in sync
To meet, to greet, intending to speak, expected to act and react and receive
To solve, to resolve and refuse to accept not to expect to make it right
To refuel for a short while in order to begin to recharge before the time comes
To rewind and begin to reverse the steps to cleverly reclaim what remains
leaving behind what was left undone; for now it can't ever be changed
To plan a retreat to return to what was left behind so loved and well known
To resolve to recoup to rethink to revisit what went unfinished or undone from today
Finally, to retire from the revolving perpetual cycle that has now made its claim
Tomorrow, we'll turn the page, redefine and recreate the steps to reinstate *then*
Get up to recycle and propel ourselves in the same motions that we'll retake once again

Blended Blues of Euphoria

Varied vibrant shades of blue passionately break through
the solid color barrier pleasantly shattering the code of purity
A perfect blend of mixtures appear to create surreal thoughts
from vague to clear, igniting an effusive spectrum of appealing hues
that can reveal real beauty but only to mine eyes, the beholder

Light powder puff shades *of blue* as they converge and descend from
wholesome blue skies
Here is where the mind awakens and conjoins with the universe
Realism ceases to exist and only transiently appears to me before
Tones of *teal* flush out a spicy scenario which gets dusted
with glistening specks *of sapphires and royals* as they rush in
with lighthearted gaiety
In an instant I feel sparks igniting in my head, touching those
innermost feelings *that crave to savor their rich variety and excitement
a charge to go forward!*
I glance toward the magically majestic *indigo* that teases and pleases
the passion creating moving moments I can hardly understand or explain
I am lightly lifted above it all, soaring to heights rising higher
to reach the apex of this sensory visual experience!
And now, I'm softly ejected by parachute into a refreshing pool
for a cool and calming *aqua* cleansing for a sensational cooldown
All that's left to claim is the intermingling of *periwinkle* and *navy*
mixed well to dissolve anything slightly out of sync with the eyes while
they continue on this self-indulging, soulful journey of the color appeal
As finality comes into view, order returns and I seek to be submerged
and drenched in the *azure* assuredness of peace and restful tranquility
This, is often the chosen sanctuary my mind so deeply desires and often finds

Lunar Mysteries

A mystique exists through the phases
in the faces of the celestial moon
continually changing
the image it shows
Nothing can contain its vibrant shine
A bright star that illuminates and captures the sight
of many gazers who are drawn to its emboldened light
Standing silently still yet appearing in countless places
all at once, a ubiquitous remote body
Where gazes of awe render speechless amazement
of its luminous and captivating glow
appearing in whole, half or crisp crescent form
dressed in shades of dazzling white to soft pale yellow,
revealing only the part of itself that wants to be seen
Prompting inquiries and conversations of bewilderment
From the abundant source of light lie answers to
questions not yet conceived
unpretentious and unsurpassed
Not ever fully known nor understood
This sphere is an entity of its own right
Journeys past have led to light-years still astray
new encounters are still paving an anonymous way
for more opportunities of promising discoveries
What more can there possibly be to know?
But so much still seems yet to be revealed
The moon possesses true mysteries of its very own

Like a Whispering Wind

As doves do fly
Tranquilly, quietly, unruffled by life's cares
They somehow find their lonesome way
Through the clouds in the sky that linger high
as they aimlessly crisscross an endless sky
No pattern or direction to charter their path
Ultimately, they find a restful place somewhere
disappearing so quietly into the soft satin pillows
Leaving a calming and comforting peace within

Deep Down Transition

The warmth of the cool water embodies my soul as it envelops me
It is the essence of who I am right now, suspended and so carefree
A virtual weightless object floating lifelessly immersed languidly
in a sea of quiet calmness
Sinking deep down to a limitless space of unmeasured time
It is here that I find warmth of this balmy experience
Filling my head completely and encompassing me in a natural
surreal scene of a bottomless plane
Without being aware, I'm swept away on a water expedition
I cruise through the deepest channel momentarily and
let my body give in to the waves that will carry me away on
the fantastic voyage deep in the Caribbean Sea,
a marvelous expedition of wonder indeed

A Squared Configuration

Thoughts fit neatly in the corners of an inspired mind
squarely fixated at the stimuli that makes its way forward
first as a hint compressed and compacted in the neatly boxed area
where random thoughts and words actively interact while
bouncing back and forth, from wall to wall, sliding into the corners
in time they are evenly shaped and precisely formed into ideas
that will be articulated first to an audience of one and then another
then released to the vast atmosphere as a brilliant or broken idea
which more or less is likely to be rejected or accepted as noteworthy

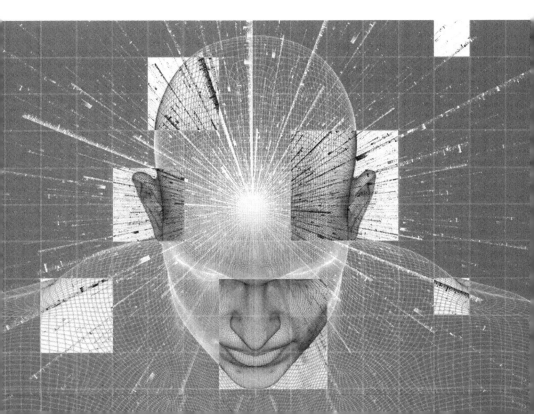

Rendezvous at the Shore

At dawn the ocean's energy awakens and beckons the foot soldiers
to its sandy shore offering up a challenge to keep pace with the sun's
rising deep golden warmth

At midday, the worshipers answer the sun's call to come and receive
generous portions of sweltering heat that heavily beats its way
through the long sweltering summer day

All that can be heard are the sounds of the water, hearty laughter
resounding in playful folly and there they leisurely lay as the hours
slip slowly away into the lazy languid afternoon

Time no longer exists and they now fight to resist, the subtle urge
to rise up and go back to seek respite from the summer sun
Instead they'll soak up the warmth as the waves continue to
come rushing forth up on the shore

Drawn to the edge at the sun's last hurrah, they return to unwind
and stroll along the calming shores that speak now in hushed tones
The quiet slow rhythm now pulsing ever so lightly as the golden beam
starts its descent and prepares to exit the scene while the sounds of the tide
saunter into the peaceful, sandy shore

All that remains in the pitch of the night is the softness of its grasp and
pleasant memories left from the day after all who were here have gone

Lasting Imprint

SAID it
MEANT it,
Won't take it BACK
NO!
THAT CAN'T BE DONE
Reverse the unwanted,
Retrieve the intractable
which has now become the unthinkable and barely understood
just a thought not intended to ever be known, heard or shared
yet it was so foolishly spoken, a heart broken, no thought of
feelings were even spared
the vocal residue hurled around, striking without hesitation
reverence or respect
shattering the cohesive connection like a sudden unpredicted storm
pushing its way into the breakthrough of the day's early morning dawn
slashing like a sword on a zigzag mission to disband and destroy
syllables that came in repetitive numbers imposing their way while
forcibly breaking through the wall of the stunned but curious mind
The impact of them was like a runaway train that rapidly rumbles
 through the tunnel at "break neck speed" in the pitch black night
rolling on the wheels of offenses determined to make their presence
known, just before relinquishing a rebellious stand...
then purposely coming to a precise HALT

What was hurled in the air so recklessly has now been
permanently recorded with no erasable ink
where memory makes its final mark on the wounded one's heart
Only through the course of time will it begin to fade
erasing the harmful stain, resigning itself to concede,
to turn back and ease itself into a slow but guarded walk away
attempting to carefully replant the seeds of peace...
Now they are stored in the annals of a time not so far away
a forgotten past where they will begin to melt away gradually
but not without first leaving a dusty print, a not so pretty picture
etched into the recollection of the ways things once were before
the vocal firestorm boldly insinuated itself into existence
But from this day on, things will never be quite the same

EXPRESSIONS 2

Admiration

Her strength is paramount to the vigor of a 6 woman rowing team
that combined their forces to conquer the brisk chilled waters
on an early Sunday morning, while navigating steadily down Charles River
on the coldest winter day

They move with the boldness and fortitude that it took Ms. Harriet
to lead bands of fearless men, women and children
on a freedom journey north, away from their oppressors
and the determination of Sister Sojourner to shame the devil
and tell the biting brittle truth to those brave enough to keep
their eyes fixed ahead on the good for all mankind

Even when faced with the strong hands of opposition
she remains stoically still like the only remaining tree
unbroken and unscathed after a fierce tumultuous storm
which swept through unforgivingly and erased almost all
but the already barren land it was left standing on

She possesses that kind of indelible strength we love and admire
That of a warrior on a long and determined journey with still many days
and nights left ahead, prepared to remain firm and free from fear
Here is where we find our reserve entrenched in her deeply caring soul
It makes us pull up, stand straight, and push fiercely on
determined to triumph, not be chiseled down or persuaded to give in
to the threats and pressures that she knows will try to claim us
because by her example, we've been trained to remain
confident that we can win, despite all odds
She will not be deterred nor made to feel to be the lesser
and nor will we!
even when knocked flat down facing the crust of the dry gritty earth
we'll get back up and move on!

She represents someone so vastly familiar and personal to us
We've seen her often in the faces of our own mothers, daughters, sisters,
and friends who make us feel proud of their undertakings and courage
to stay in the race until the very end

Always gracefully wearing the appearance of undeniable beauty and strength,
she possesses an invincible spirit that always shines and promises to
repeat itself endlessly through time

Tribute to Fathers

Salute to you, fathers
Fathers, who have gone on before us and are now
loving us from their eternal resting places
Fathers, who thankfully have been returned to us from the
ravages of war, dues paid far beyond what could ever be imagined
or for a debt you never made or ever owed
You deserve to always be honored at home and away

We are grateful to you fathers, those who have come back
home after passing through the revolving door of incarceration
determined to preserve the existence of the family
not to leave it broken or in eternal disrepair
and those who strayed away for reasons unknown or not ever
mentioned but stepped back in for the good of their children
and sometimes for the women they still cared for and loved

Stand to give a resounding applause for those who have even tried
to rewind the hands of long lost time
only to discover too late that it was futile
to reach back for the dream now forever deferred

Dear Father above, we pray for all fathers who have chosen to protect
and provide and not to procrastinate and then pivot quietly away
from the road paved with gold where riches will unfold one day

Hail to you fathers for the unwavering commitment to leave a worthy
legacy which will be carried on to honor your heritage and the name
you so proudly claim and the extraordinary sacrifice of immeasurable love
you unfailingly rendered to your children asking for little or nothing in return
It's stronghold is held close to our hearts and forever etched in our minds

A Modest Prayer for the New Generation

Bowed humbly before the Almighty power
offering a simple prayer for all youth today
Keep them safe, so that they won't stumble and perish
on life's road as it twists and bends along their way
A prayer that their paths be made discernibly clear
that they hold hands with faith and hope
take the journey without thoughts of fear
To strive for good health by far their greatest wealth
and keep family and close friends always near
Give them a saving grace for their protection
Let them walk not by their own plain sight
forsake the evil at all costs and embrace
what they know to be honest and right
To you, we make this earnest heartfelt plea
to help them through their toughest times
so that they can know contentment and each day feel free
You know what they want, provide what you know they need
Always be by their side to guide while they chase their
youthful restless dreams that to them right now
seem destined to become a guaranteed reality
At last, reveal to them a pathway that is emblazoned with light
that will lead them by day and then carry on through the hours
of their darkest nights

The Gift

Life is a lovely present
A very precious gift
Carefully packaged and wrapped
A regal joy that's meant to
covet, savor, and protect
And if not carefully watched and kept
will elusively slip away and vanish
before you can appreciate its beauty
and experience its fullest joy!

Regret Full

When you say "I'm sorry" does that mean you're *really* sad
to have caused another person pain or made someone mad
or are you just sorry to have to release those words instead?
evoking a biting reminder of the unpleasant words that were said

The dimensions of a heartless sorry have no defined lines for a remedy
tumbling instead like a reckless weed dropped carelessly into a bottomless pit
left turning over and over with no real end, so that they can no longer
be retrieved from the moving drift that will eventually claim their existence
Hurtful words plunged deep into imaginary walls of no return
then left abandoned to travel aimlessly alone down a one-way street
where they will simply "hang out" until it no longer matters anymore
An unfelt sorry is so vastly empty and so void of feeling,
left wandering alone, where can those words possibly go?
Have you ever considered the impact or the toll they will take
on the heart that has been ripped and torn and left to manifest
in the negative realm so long?
Nothing changed, restored or no victory even won
and so there they remain to fester and rotten, blazing and burning inside
The words themselves thrashing about and leaving their scathing sting
on the badly wounded heart and the clear conscious mind
But no longer does it matter to the heart that can't feel
or to the deafened ear that no longer hears what it says
Can it really be that the remorseful plea has been rejected and
turned back to the place from where it came or
making an attempt to cash in and be redeemed erasing the slate clean until
it happens once again?

Would the words that were so thoughtlessly uttered just have been better left unsaid?

Looking Outward

It's pleasant to take a view of life at times from the inside to the out
Stand and glare from where the view is woven tightly through intricate doors
What exists is a quiet and soothing tranquility of its hardest molten core
Stay fixed in place and enjoy the cool and calm to soothe the weariest searching soul
It's protected from the blight that exists just outside the world's darkest veil
What lies beyond the curtain just on the other side is a painful depiction
which can't be seen through our self-adjusted rose colored lenses
Standing on the other side, the viewpoint clearly reverses itself

Shaken out, it gives way from the firm hold for a chance to see
the "real of things" as it is throughout, void of even the slightest doubt
Stepping away cautiously from a self-created comfort zone and
left alone to face the reality at what can be plainly seen and known,
the jolt sifts out the good and allows an awakening truth to come in
The mind tries to cling to the surreal formed from a sense of pride
but quickly transforms to the configuration of what exists on the flip side

Dreams abruptly crushed and destroyed by lies, unfairness, and envy
wedged between people of all races, creed, and nationality all the while
further widening the fragile lines of separation against all of humanity
They fester and run amok, threatening to surge out of control with infestation
Harmony can't ever exist in any form of cohesive totality for a civil society

Instead, let love and peace flow like a stream into the hearts of all mankind
This is the truth we want to find when we finally emerge from the other side.

What Resonates in Your Soul?

Do you hear your inner voice calling out your name
to hold on to what you may not clearly see now?
It's telling you to just simply stand firm on what you believe
Solid faith formed as the substance of what you really need
No matter how bleak it presently seems or even how
hopeless things may appear to be
Don't give in to the doubts that muddle your mind
Keep pedaling so defiantly upstream in search of the dream
that you'll eventually find
When persistent bad thoughts seemingly can't be released
flowing from day to day, preventing many nights of sleep
Stand firm and continue to remain solidly fixed in place
soon the dark will pass on and you'll realize that you have received
the amazing gift of grace

Can you somewhere feel the promise of a sweet serenity
bellowing from that faraway place you hold deep inside?
Its voice affixed and held so tight by your constantly churning mind
willing you not to give up, it won't be long, echoing its worth in kind
seeking to reveal itself one day after the rocky waves calm down
Soon that promise will reach out and take a firm hold of your
praying hands, then the newness will spark fresh ideas to
help you journey on once again
So listen to the relentless voice that calls with a refusal to
retreat from the place where it has chosen to take a firm stand
Reignite your fighting spirit, believe in that inner voice,
that continues to tell you that "You Can"!

Unruly Crown

You can roll it, curl it, brush it, and even try to plait it
but dare not try to smooth it down or attempt to try to wrap it
It just won't happen in a quick snap
Nap won't wrap like that - without some divine intervention
a warm iron or a strong permanent solution
to make it cower and yield, to conform to the unreal,
and give it long-lasting appeal you so desire
But Why?
just to bring about a change that you can live with for an oh so
moment in time, to not be your true self, there is no reason or rhyme
At what cost have you then altered your natural mane
and then what was the price you had to pay?
when you gave in and relinquished your original given beauty
that otherwise should never have to be sacrificed or modified,
not even for a moment should you think you need to compromise
just to sport an unoriginal and less indigenous look that leads to
a diversion into a murky digression from your own true heritage
a betrayal of your lovely birthright and proud ethnicity
just to have hair that is more popular, and yes... even more widely
accepted by the masses, the greater society, that dictates what
should really matter to you and to me
but to this, I admit that I just can't submit!
Instead, I choose to remain firmly fixed on accentuating
my own natural gift, so full of richness and versatility!

The Heart of the Soul

Knocks with a pounding unrelenting knock that
is not molded or limited by pure flesh and blood
Instead it is woven in synchronized, syncopated beats,
marching to a precise accented rhythm
A perfectly running engine that can ignite the body's
emotional gauge and read it in split second beats
It may momentarily stop to cry, to mourn and feel the ache,
to laugh, or pick up its throb at the right time to celebrate
Then it resumes its cadence, regains its role to get back on course
and continue beating steadily on with unnoticed precision
designed to stay precisely in step, not a stroke is missed
an amazing instrument encased in every human soul
It will always keep pace with the unconscious mind
as new thoughts and feelings continue to flow

A to F Sharp#

Give me a melody to the lonesome words of my beautiful prose
A tempo to go happily along with my rhythmic highs and languid lows
Can you give my ear a tune to go in perfect sync with what my mind
already seems to know?
I'm sure a harmony can be born to make us just right for one another
matched like a flawless duo
Release the right chords to turn my succinct thoughts into the perfect song
One that can be liked and sung throughout the day and even as the night lingers on
Bellow out the base that will pick up the pace for what I've composed because
these lyrics can no longer stand alone
I'm certain they won't hang around much longer without a companion and a home

De-Selection

Excuse me please, step to the side, while I push the right button
to deselect all negativity that taints and spoils all that is good and better
Step back for a moment, while I deposit them into a refuse to be
thrown away forever
I choose to deselect envy because it secretly harbors resentment
and utter bitterness
Hatred, because it holds a monster that severely damages and
leaves a mark that can never be truly erased, but rather it remains as
a leftover, a reminder of the dreadful result it made

Instead, I choose that which is right for all in order to live in
peace and harmony
I'll pay the full price at whatever the cost, just let my selection
not be pushed aside, squandered or somehow lost
My desire is to embrace and nurture that which manifests good
until it spreads throughout like a virus in a confined space moving
quickly one to another without the limits of discrimination
The selection for me indeed won't be one to inflict pain and harm
which will only sound off the alarm leaving us wanting for something
more than a scathing scar left on the arms of humanity
Let me push the button that doesn't despise but drops down love,
compassion and care, not just here but we need it so much everywhere
The world could use more packaged "good" rather than the evils that
are already lurking maliciously in secret places out there
Surplus boxes of bad have been well prepared so when chosen they
quickly start to overtake what was made to be worthy of care
negating a chance to have the good choices most likely to be craved
Pick up the bag of niceties and better treatment for an unexpected change
Believe me, these chosen goods won't even cost you a single thing
Taste a sample of what could be shared and enjoyed by all if only
for goodness' sake nothing more
Make a choice to deselect that which will ultimately lead to our certain demise
For if we don't choose to do it now, the toll on humanity will continue to rise
I want to insert my coins in the slot to make my selection at this time
Excuse me please, while you're still thinking about it, and step aside

First Place Losers

Who really wins in times of senseless war?
Each side robbed of its self-proclaimed right for normalcy
When lives are lost and dreams are severely decimated
Everybody loses and no victory can be rightly celebrated
When raging days drag into longer lonely anguished nights
left from the agony and suffering, from the hell-raising fights
There are no winners who can step up with exaltation and cheer
to hold up the banner that has forever been marred by pain from fear
The losers all emerge together hardly free from battle scars that will
remain to be seen, bearing the badges of blood and toil, changed
because they answered the call and handed over their dignity
in exchange for a game of total loss from death and destruction
All in all, too much of a price to pay
and nothing left but disgust and shame

Interlocked

From the heart of a man
From the strength of a woman
Grows the fruit of love's labor
Perplexed at the splendor of the moment
when new life appears, it's a wonderment indeed
Sweet memories are made at the moment of birth
that will be fondly cherished for many years
The mystery of the creation of new life is tenderly
held as secrets interlocked in their intertwined hearts
As if they will ultimately be revealed one day

Slippers

Tread carefully on the rocky road ahead
paved mainly with colorful smooth stones
Each step may lead to a maze of a tempting snare
where life's trouble stalks and awaits you there
to take ownership of your wanting soul and leave you reeling
with true despair
An upheaval indeed, like riding in a rocking boat
through the eye of a storm with no way to see
blinded while in search of bits and pieces of calm

Instead walk gently and take caution with every stride you make
with your eyes firmly fixed on the road that lies ahead
no warning signs will wave a hand or likely greet you at the gate
Have the presence of mind and the courage of heart to confront
the rocks that fall onto your path, as the uneven road with its heavy
load will turn you around in search of another way to get back

Mysteries will be discovered and secrets before you will unfold
In time their purposes will be made clear, the truth revealed and told

An Angel's Touch

When angels walk among us, we seldom know they're here
Instead we simply understand that God is standing very near
Rendering his love and mercy, quelling our deepest fears
They touch our hearts in special ways and bring us calm and cheer
What they do to ease our pain, relieves sadness from our sorrow
This leaves us with rekindled hopes
the promise of brighter days tomorrow
But most of all, when angels leave us, our hearts are less burdened
and we are never again the same; so we look above to render thanks,
glad that an angel chose our name

Jack-y

Cool and calm a boy named Jack
He's really such a cute lil chap
He turns and smiles at me
Yeah! and then that is that
My heart begins to quickly pound
I feel it lift and flip then spin around
Right then without a single doubt
I declare my feelings for him from the inside out
Too soon I give in to his little childish whims
Which makes my adoration begin to transcend
It's a joy to be with him, both day and night
He's happy and bright, which makes it so all right
You can call him my man for sure and that's a fact
Oh, by the way, did I mention it before?
We call him Jack!

Take the Ride

Take the oar and row your boat gently in and out of life's stream
for what awaits from day to day is not known but meant to be
At times you'll find you're gliding steadily through the
soft and mellow winds
And while you ponder the new direction you should take
you'll get thrusted unexpectedly into the torrent winds
Sometimes you'll sail over the waves and handle life's challenges
with a breeze
but when the waters are really rough you may feel tossed
and blown about like leaves
Whether you're being dropped down deep into the current that
always seems to flow
or paddling your way to stay on the course wherever the wind
doth want to blow
You've been signed up for an unforgettable experience on the
greatest ride of your life!

Burst of Purple

Purple passion
Passion flows
Flows forever
to hearts that glow
Purple Passion
Purple Pain
Flowers Bloom
From Purple Rain
Hope regenerated
Alas, here we do sing
Spring joyfully arrives
To bring new life again

Shared Day by Birth

We stand together like a pair
to acknowledge our connection
namely the day of birth we share
Traits we see to be strong in ourselves
are seen as solid in each other as well
not easily annoyed by slights and the
insignificant smaller things of life
undeterred always from pursuing
dreams and the goals we seek to reach
choosing our own path to walk and
not follow the one we clearly see
believing in ourselves is what we know
true to ourselves is all we want to show
This day won't be marred or scarred
today is our shared time to celebrate
this occurrence of who we know we are
and why fate brought us here together
especially on this day

Up Right Down

How is it that we can live contently in a world so upside down
Confusing the wrongs negating what should be right
What will it take to make it correct in our sight?
Embracing the embarrassing
Disowning the downtrodden
Uplifting the self-serving
but condemning the compassionate
for caring about what really should matter
Crafted and skewed by so many false pretenses
we choose to approve of the absurd behavior
that is the most seemingly distasteful
checking it off as one of our favorites
Give it a new sticker and label it routine and norm
Yet we can't find a way to adopt the good morals
which are something we should condone
Flip the page, turn it all around, we can improve
what we feel by looking up from the ground
Imagine how differently things could be seen inverted
If given a way to improve our outlook with a fresh perspective
Regenerated smiles can be brought back around
when the sadness of a frown is no longer fixed
in its gloomy place looking down

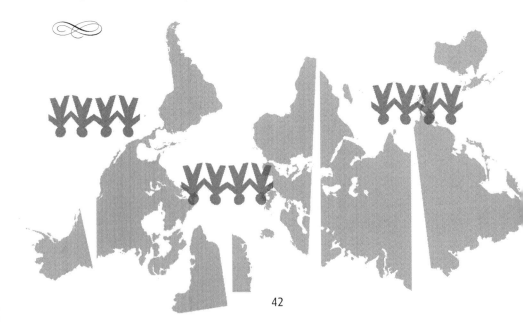

A Right to Be Free

Just like the trapped bird, I long to be so fancy free
to chart a new path and live out my chosen destiny
Don't try to keep me locked in, held down, detained or caged
I know I'll fester in that space and soon become so enraged
Rendering me unable to freely spread my wide open wings
I'll turn my attention up to the stars with a song I've
so longed to sing
My yearning is to fly far from here and soar so high with glee
Let me discover some distant places
I only know right now in my happy dreams
I'm ready to make my claim to what I've waited for so long
to try and see what's right for me, I yearn for so much more
Tomorrow I'll shed my melancholy and wait to make my way
I'll give flight to the wind, just over the bend, at dawn's
first break of day
After seeing darkness slowly fading into the early morning's light
I'll turn my face toward the sun seeking a path not yet clearly
in my clouded sight
When all is calm and quiet and the cage door is finally left ajar
I'll take my chance and fly away seeking what lies out there afar
Once there I'll gladly rejoice singing loud my newly found freedom's song
and resolve never to be confined that way again especially for so long

Remembering JE

Different by description
Fun-loving by nature
Talented by design, yet
Unaccepted by too many
Locked in a lifestyle before its time
Mainstream too straight to understand
No place here for the "others" they said
So much unanswered and many wrongly misjudged
Forced to remain the same, concealed, denying his truth
Swept up in the current of liberal sexual madness
Fell prey to the plague that was feared by the masses
Only a memory remains now of what could not then be
Gone much too soon and missed by many, but now
He's finally free!

Sunset's Solace

Cast your worries and cares to the slow setting sun

Relinquish them with the passing day, let them go one by one

Don't let them take a firm hold of the ole strong and mighty sword

and root themselves while standing so firm at fertile ground's door

For that time has gone and is no more, leaving only its permanent stain

It can't be recalled, remade, invisibly erased, it will always remain unchanged

But tomorrow's potential of something unknown and new, will ignite a spirit to

answer the call, go on a new path, seeking a better way if you so solemnly choose

Pressing its mark for the privilege and promise for a way that's paved with light

and voicing the gratefulness for another day and a chance to make it right

Mind Detox

Meditate thoughtfully
Find your focal point
Fix your purpose on it
Massage your psyche
Purge the damaged
Repel the unwanted
And refuse to accept it anymore
Look forward to a better life
Awaiting behind an unknown door
Just beyond the wall that will fall
Could be what you've been yearning for
Walk firmly toward your unfinished goal
Keep the wind always pressing at your back
Prepare to reclaim your stolen dreams
Push forward and try to stay on track
Resolve to live in the present for now
Leave the old and unpleasant far behind
Relax and go forward with hope and faith
Taking one measured step at a time

Speak On It!

Never got enough cash but getting by okay
Trying to get ahead by making an honest way
Tired of being a dollar short at the end of the day
Not really complaining, but I'm just here saying

Treading carefully along the narrow edge and back
Hope lies beyond what can be seen and known as fact
That thin line will surely disappear if you slip and fall back
Maintain your footing and stay focused, it will be alright

Keep on going and make it work is what I mean
Been there, done that, and even some things in between
Rainy days do come, cause they can't be wished away
Not complaining at all, hey listen, I'm just saying

Can't keep a steady pace without being in the rapid race
Rolling along life's roads hoping all dreams will somehow
fall in place
Why can't it be, to me, as it seems should be the simple case
You conceive, then proceed, it manifests because you believe
What's the problem here, when will the harvest start to pay?
Don't think for a moment that I'm here venting or complaining
but the truth MUST be told... and I'm just saying!

True Sisters

Joined not by blood or any natural birthright
Yet our lives are entwined in many intricate ways
Separated by distance, family, and our chosen careers
Yet never out of touch with one another over the course of years
Lifestyles are parallel and reflect the decisions of our choices
Not always expressing our thoughts and feelings
but forever hearing each other's silent voices
and knowing that we're always here for one another
The tie that binds can't be broken by distance or time
Friendship solidified like the Olympic rings that intertwine
Continuously linked and joined in true alliance
Blue minds stilled in peace envelope us
Green fertile paths we travel develop us
Yellow bright spirits easily lift and inspire us
Red hearts that are true will forever unite us
Black Sisters joined in harmony is who we are!

This Special Day

Hands come together at the altar to pray
Hearts bonded now forever marked as a joyful day
Vows solemnly made in truth, faith, and love
Witnessed fondly by many family and friends
Sanctioned and blessed by God from above
Hope for years of joy and true happiness is said
Choosing to unite, together they've chosen a new path
Today is so purposed as written in the book of life
Man and Woman have now joined as husband and wife

Whisper of the Voiceless

Who's going to speak for the homeless
with nothing and nowhere to go
Who will hear the voices of the hungry
as their painful stories continue to go untold
How can the helpless cry out when their
words are so limp with unspoken shame
Overshadowed by the rhetoric of those who
speak many words but never try to feel their pain
Who will speak for the hopeless and nameless
abandoned by those who didn't have time to care
Where are we going in such a rush that we leave them
far behind, silently crying for some help while slowly dying inside
Why don't we turn ourselves toward their solemn faces
forgetting the lines that divide gender, creed, and races
Instead, let's incline our hearts to hear their cries
and begin addressing what they really need
Pick up the torch, step up to answer the call and
follow those who whole-heartedly take the lead
When will we stop hurling so much scorn and blame
knowing that those silent cries we don't hear are out there
somewhere calling out our names

What will it take?

REFLECTIONS

Saturn's Mystical Unveiling

*Rings of brown smooth chocolate
allowing light to transcend between
herself and the world beyond as we know it
She exists from where thoughts of truth is brushed with
melancholy
a wonderment of mystery to be unraveled in time
that was observed from being in her company
Just one quick gaze, then another, lingering just long
enough to stop the intrusion of doubt before turning away
in wonder
What is met just beyond that point is beauty and loveliness
They exist conjointly, precisely fixed in place and wrapped in
layers of pleasantry and a warm personality
They convey a silent message that invites you to
discover the beauty that lies deep within by taking the time
needed to get to really know her
What dwells in those eyes is a priceless love of life
filled with a mystical charm
that can never be truly translated into words*

The Day Before

Skies were clear with hues of blue,
unmarked by anything unknown or new
like the daily routine firmly set in place
There it was then as it had always been
tasks established and followed each day
like the steady precision of the hands on a
wall-mounted clock with a pulsing pendulum
swinging back and forth
in a precise and continuous motion
its destiny set to strike a prediction
of some sameness every hour
as an arrow aiming straight for the bull's eye
destination ahead, moving in slow motion

Then came you and everything changed
All that mattered before just
stood up and walked away

Suddenly, there you were set permanently on the scene
emerging from the depths of somewhere not known
appearing unannounced clothed in some anonymity
fixed on a mission to change the course and direction
waiting from behind the scene just before the
curtain's final call

A coincidental event birthing itself in one quick unsuspecting
twinkling that could not have been known at even a moment before
now molded and set as a permanent fixture held firmly in place
bringing with you a new spirit that moved in perfect sync and linked
so perfectly right for that coveted time thus rendering a renaissance
of thought about how things were supposed to be but had not been
before now

Restful Moments

The meditation of my heart includes memories of you
Your voice's deep sound that now resounds in my mind
A fragment of your face with eyes that sharply pierced mine
As we sat so placidly at the window one summer afternoon
There is where we discovered life's truth though frayed and
glazed with only half truths that held us in suspended imagination
Even now as days pass into nights and your visage lingers in place
unanswered questions and answers uncontested encircle my mind
But my heart remains a separate entity on a course of its own
It yearns to revisit the past frequently in search of who you were
and ponders how and why you just so suddenly slipped away

Our "Oui" (We) Time

On Valentine's Day Eve, just a little before midnight
we'll stop and stargaze out into the dark skylight
where time has no meaning to actualize or claim our existence
just you and me lovingly lingering in our infinite undefined space
In this time "Oui" will search our hearts for a taste of contentment
that we'll find embedded in some temporary moments of suspended reality
and maybe for an instant, we will suddenly stop to reflect and realize
that something has eluded us in that space where we stood before now
Then maybe, we'll consciously choose to linger there awhile longer
embraced in each other's arms on a night especially made for lovers

The Task of Time

The nameless of the sameness
craftily carves its signature
to create a world of its own
It captures the least suspecting
even the much revered all knowing
then sweeps them solidly together
into a mundane stream of simplicity
which solemnly manifests itself
in the endless passing of time
Each moment is not always
deserving of recognition or merit
yet every millisecond is undeniably
implanted in that which can't be
ceased or changed
from dawn's first light to
dark's nocturnal sight
Time never stops to pause or rest
or contemplate a moment to reflect
instead, continually claiming its own
as it remains on a steady course
destined to fulfill its ultimate goal
And we, its subjects
are obviously left behind
solely to measure the permanent mark
it makes, after it has come and gone

Warm Expectation

Just after the break of dawn's early hour,
I sauntered easily into the crowd
Moving steadily without reservation,
reluctant hesitation or guilt

I knew I had to be early, for perhaps this just one chance
to capture the magic of the moment that I was sure this
encounter would surely bring
My pace quickened, I wanted to stay on course
hastening to my desired destination
so I tried not to fall back and lose time
but continued to focus and press on
to linger on the promise soon to be

I looked around, then back for one split second more
yet identified no one in the crowd, not a friendly face or foe
and so continued to what was relentlessly calling me
a quest, a mission, to experience perhaps true satisfaction
I longed to know but now with more determination to go
happily fulfill my heart's most sincere desire
I steadied myself on the path I would take
For I knew that I had to go and didn't want to be late
I had no choice except to be there soon, to see,

As I came closer to the arrival time, my heart began to race and
I took one last glance down the street, of course, just in case
I knew what lay ahead for me was far beyond the current scene
Daring to ponder the unknown encounter not yet revealed
I paused for just a moment to peer into a mirror at my probing soul
Unexpectedly, appearing there inside the looking glass was something
that clearly reflected the yearning inside of the inner me
which to now had long awaited to be captivated tenderly

Stepping into the threshold, I was already feeling a desire to remain
and accept the offer to partake of the warmth that greeted me
An invitation extended, to sit and chit the chat awhile
to reflect, exchange thoughts and ideas, to gaze and smile

I'll cherish those long awaited moments of well-spent time
that brisk cold day in December savored and remembered
for the good conversation and warm cups of cappuccino
I was able to enjoy that morning with my secret lover

Journey

Leaving now would release me from the need for a reason
to explain where I'm going or why I must check out for awhile
since that uncertain mystery is still drawing me secretly closer
to some unidentified place not yet revealed to anyone, not even me

Somehow it's vaguely familiar in its existence and form
but is still lacking a destination and revelation of its true identity
I'm certain to find my way there, though the location still unknown
a safe haven far away beckons to me and awaits my presence
At the point of departure, I feel a gentle force quietly pulling my
heart along for company as a passenger on this mystical expedition
where perhaps my unrevealed fortune awaits

I'm connected and committed to this cosmic calling and yearn to know
what fanciful experience lies ahead for me
My only need is to be finally free of the undesirable forces that are always
compelling me to stay positioned here, out of place, trying to keep pace,
but somehow lost in real time

When I can no longer resist and delay the unwavering urge to answer the call to go,
I prepare my mind and look forward to this expedition of unexplored amazement
As I set out on this obscure mission chosen by my own submission
I let go and let it lead me willingly astray, unknowing that when
I suddenly awake in only a few minutes from now,
realizing that I've only been momentarily suspended
in a hazy world of some reverie and thoughtless daydream
creatively formed from my own imagination, I'll have no
desire to be drawn back too soon to the reality that I so easily left behind

Stolen (by Alzheimer's Disease)

I remember my dad he was reaally baaad!!
not vile or full of selfish deeds or dangerous dares
but there because we knew his heart, he really cared
about the happiness and joy that others could have
So it made me so sad when he checked out without notice
One day, he decided to go leaving me here all alone
All I wanted to know... was why and where had he gone?
I was left to ponder his absence spoken so loudly and really heard
a temporary stay at first, for just one day, to a time somewhere in his past
I was certain it would not last, so I waited patiently for his safe return
It was there that he lingered for days, weeks and then beyond,
at brief times coming back, but only temporarily checking in and signing on
His bags were packed, all closets empty, task left undone
something yet to be defined, I knew something was wrong
and began to understand that he would not be here with me for very long
Attempts to reach him failed because he wasn't available when I called
No reply received, it was hard to believe, not even a message
was left on my phone
Now I was faced with the bitter truth, he wouldn't be back
he had finally left home
off to a place that I surely didn't know
How would I reach him at this new location
this was real, not a chosen vacation
Had he decided to take this journey by himself and make it on his own
He slipped into an empty room, to a world that was bare and strangely unknown,
bought a one-way ticket there, where he would remain, his baggage unclaimed
in a place so far away that I surely couldn't go
like the room in the back of an old vacant house, seemingly abandoned
without thought or care
or the hollow area below the stairs, where no one thinks to look,
or dares to ever tread
I knocked, but he wouldn't let me in, nor would he come out
to hear what I had to say even though
I stood waiting patiently in vain for his return to the world
where he would know me once more
But he was gone this time, forever

His Rod and Staff

Really do
send comfort to me
when I let my worries get too near
and threaten to topple my stable balance
destroy my equilibrium,
and sideswipe my symmetry
instead
They hold me close to him
just as I feel my fall from grace
as fear moves closer to diminish
my hope so that I won't see the beam
that will lighten the path which will
lead me to greener pastures
That is when I reach out for their comfort
and manage to hold on for a while longer

3:17 am

No one can truly understand the possibilities of the mindless mind
that surface long after everything is still and traps you in a phantom time
It silently creeps in and lays in waiting to waken you with sudden surprise
that nonexistent world of no reality, claiming you before you feel ready to rise
It can linger there for quite a while and claim any measure of accountability
because a captured restless soul, doesn't really know, where to go, or what to be
Existing in that undefined space, it claims no point, no purpose, or place
Just for that unclaimed time, let go and unwind, and decidedly leave it all behind
Allow the imagination to be the master of whatever it wants to conceive
Decide to relinquish your thoughts to the universe, allowing them to become
deeply immersed in a virtual pool of whatever is detached from a world of care
Take a ride and drift with the flow to a place you'd like to go
There is where you'll see that time doesn't matter, because it doesn't exist
Yes, everything else can wait until you awaken and return

Real Truths

I can find myself if left alone in my own space
to query my mind then conjure up my inner voice
to command it to speak to what needs to be said
set the record right and get it straight this time
Taking a quick but needed break from the hurried pace
I'll go far out on a limb, let go, and let the truth be told

Tears Unleashed

Where do tears go that are never freed from the eyes to which they cling?
Do they just stand still waiting patiently to drop, into a steep descent unseen
or remain sheltered and postured to be caught and ultimately spared
from the predictable plunge should they fall and crash
Or will they wait instead, protected by eyes that stand like
opened umbrellas held by people gathered tightly together at the
bus stop on a chilly, gloomy, rainy day
standing ready to catch the drops that threaten to silently fall upon them
anticipating that they will receive a free ride away from the sadness
that first brought them there, unwillingly and often unprovoked
as if they've been supplanted as sturdy substances inside
in position ready to pack up and go, but with nowhere to flow
no real objective selected or a new place to call home
At that point before they take their fall, they ponder a peaceful resolution
and begin to compress into compartmentalized pieces
that will determine their resolve and silently release themselves
discretely into the atmosphere, as micro bits interlocked in time

If / Then

If a smile brings warmth then my eyes will absorb the heat
If a touch gives pleasure then I know my heart will steadily beat
If friendship fosters happiness then my life is better because of you

Enlightened Awakening

In prayer I asked for my heart's desire and as I waited
I was given ample time to see old things angled differently
A new perspective began to slowly unfold and my heart
slowly opened like a descending parachute over a meadow
Fresh sensations sparked my brain and new hope was infused

Then times got hard and my hopeful expectation began fading away slowly
So, I asked again, this time to find contentment in what I had left
although frayed and fractured from the weariness I knew all too well
A joyful lift tugged at my heart, releasing renewed hope and fine particles of
patience began to shower upon me, as if quietly descending from nowhere
A sense of comfort came over me and gently took my hand leading me into
the illumination of light opening my blinded eyes to the previously unseen
Time had reshaped the situation and some unnamed difference had taken place
Gradually, I realized that I had already received that which I yearned for so long...
an inner peace

The Sparrow and Me

I watch it from afar as it scurries around throughout the day
I ponder at its ease of confidence moving so unassumingly away
It seemingly shows no concern or care
Whether busy around the ground
or flying away high in the air
or even when just scampering away to return to its comfy lair
When the fierce winds do come and certainly doth blow
it seeks shelter in the trees and seems unfettered by rain or snow
No matter what the weather it always finds a protected place to go
It moves so freely around its prey that's often nearby lurking in its way
Still it continues gathering food that's been provided
as if it seems to know that it would be there but just can't say
Then I stop and ponder that all its needs some way are simply met
Nothing is left undone to give it cause for worry or even a reason to fret
So why should I even feel burdened about what I'll eat or wear tomorrow
or where I'll get the resources to avoid a lot of sorrows
Each day is secure as it rests firmly in capable hands indeed
Even when I'm filled with doubt or fear and scarcely made aware
everything I've always needed has been provided somehow, somewhere
The latter leaves me awed as I start to look beyond what I can plainly see
I take a moment to stop, reflect and think what this really means
If he watches over the least with so much less
then why would he not provide for me?

No One Quite Like You

The world would be a better place
if only there were more people like you
Someone to always care and share in our lives
Making things that are old seem incredibly new
You made an ordinary occasion special
first by your mere presence alone
The hearty laughter as we gathered
resonated heartily throughout my home
Happiness and joy encircled the air
gladness was felt just because you were there
As time drifts away and we say goodbye as we part
the memory you brought will always lift up my heart
With all of the joys and despite the unwanted tears
the gift of your true unfailing friendship
will linger on sweetly throughout the coming years

Giving Plentiful Thanks

Thanksgiving is a time for reflection of what has been
gratefully received everything that is so generously given
a reason for existence, your purpose for your living
But what exactly is precious to which you hold so dear
all that is worthy of your time and care, which you keep near
Is it the valuables you possess or aspire to one day attain
or perhaps the beautiful places that you desire to see once again
or the people you love and long for, the time that you all share
What do you truly value in life, how much do you really care
Material things will fade and go as surely as they have come
Time changes everything we know when the race is over and won
So it's the true blessings of life which we should see for ourselves
Give thanks for family and friends and for the wealth of good health
then hold on to it as a treasure for it's a blessing in itself
These are the things that give true meaning to the word Thanks
as we know it should be

Iris' Eyes

Are in search of what is wrapped in mystery and waits to be sought and probed
They go to places behind hidden spaces to find more of what's there to know
Her eyes discreetly scan at the perfect point and time, to pierce precisely
through the surface to find more that lies secretly behind

They go in search of the invisible to unravel what yet remains to be seen
Where other's eyes dare to trespass, Iris' eyes will gladly go with ease
There they find a quiet place of revelation sometimes nestled neatly in between

A moment of truth to know or a consequence to gain, is the price to pay for more
Something will always draw them further in or tightly close the windowless door

When the need to know calls and captures her rapt attention
Iris' eyes will feel the lure to go and kindly accept the invitation

Mood Masters

The magic of music can shift bad moods to new levels
and place them on new and different planes
It will ease the mind and soothe the exhausted weary soul
when it's depleted of vitality and needs to be temporarily rescued
When I find myself losing ground I search for music to throw me a
life jacket of spiritual revolution

I anticipate that it will usher in the soft and soothing or vigorously vibrant colors
of sound that will bring back life when the drain that the steady grind has left my
fuel gauge on low, almost void of a supply of energy
which will offer the gift of a quick remedy of rejuvenation

The flow of music syncs itself down into the backdrop of a long weathered day
creating a longing that yearns to remain there for as long as it takes to
recoup from the liveliness that was slowly siphoned from me

So I rest awhile and revel in the expectation of a resurgence of a clear mind and
refreshed soul, my body soon to be relaxed and recharged
My senses feast on the variety of sounds as they surge then ebb into the flow
The company of elation arrives and begins to replenish my nearly empty vessel
I'm sure I don't want to return to the familiarly faux world, I chose to exit not
long ago

Rhythmic beats take control of my hands and feet and carry me pleasantly along
on a breezy journey akin to inhaling fresh air in a red convertible while casually
riding through a city street on a warm but not so humid summer's night

Unending high energy resurfaces to transform my mood now to new heights
where it's met by bright colors clashing in joyful scintillating motions then
ultimately deposits me into a calming mellow pool of real relief
Then I begin a slow countdown and settle with the satisfaction that this
healing respite was what I really needed hours ago

Guitar Bandit

Quietly snatched from her resting place
where she had stood silently for so long
leaning so leisurely against the comfortable chair
by the wall in the occupied room upstairs
Taken from a corner on a rainy afternoon
when a whimsical mood inflicted a faint thought
and wonderment of what she could be someday
If her strings were strummed and stroked
then coaxed into creating some beautiful notes
that could blend casually into cascading chords
That cadence certainly would soon connect with others
that were compatible to her sound to create favorable
songs that would emerge from the depths of some talented minds
Together they could create a song never heard of before
or remake one so pleasantly familiar that they could perform
knowing that the words had been felt first in the heart then willed by
hands and fingers to come along on a magical musical journey
rendering a so smooth blended melody or jolting rendition
And so, as it was meant to be, it was now happening,
at a vibrant jazz session one late evening

Now, she's here for the gathering at the chosen venue
because some have come to hear the resonant sounds from the strings,
the horns and wood that will descend and release pleasantry to their ears
Tonight, the crowd will be aroused and applaud again and again
Cheers will be given to the one that once stood silently alone and
abandoned in the corner of the not so empty room at the top of the stairs
before finally being swept away and made to be played once again

Twelve Empty Vases

There they stand on the highest shelf in the room silenced now only by the hands of time
They once held assorted arrangements of beautiful flowers that sang their sweet melodies
Played over and over again and again touching every tiny corner of a sentimental heart
Each one has its own story that is still savored, begging never to be forgotten
The appealing and vividly familiar that always awakened the placid senses by
the colorful array of heartfelt words they conveyed so sweetly each time they arrived
They etched their signature softly and now are buried deep in treasured memories
The roses that aroused the senses in fragrant flashes of bright reds and pink
And too true were the tulips that appealed to the mixed media of one's imaginative side
blended petals of hues that rendered a radiant rainbow made to impress more than
Less forget me not, the purple passions that briefly bloomed to speak their meaning
And the merry marigolds bursting through excitedly bringing more warmth
into the lazy summer's day even after they had dried and were set aside, retained as a keepsake
for potpourri after many weeks had gone by, no song was ever left unsung…
In the fall, warm foliage slowly sauntered in dawning perfect picturesque pansies and
complementing earthy mixtures of hearty mums that sat on the step outside where they would
signal a reminder that there was something to be embraced in the cold winter season to come
As the year waned to its end and winter's harsh hand blustered, carnations countered
the beauty of the cold period with more sentimental stories of nature's mark of beauty
To each its own, new joys, a heart of hope, shards and sparks of the tender side of life
Every one of them somehow fitted perfectly in clear cylinders of varied sizes and shapes
which are now transparent and empty, standing still in silence many years later
holding them in their places

REVELATIONS 4

Hazy Perceptions

You'll find her mind searching for specks of Magenta to temper the
rigid lines of a black and white domain
She sees less pigmented shades of wrong, evil and despair
a view of some uncertainty that would not skew her realism
but rather one that would reveal an actuality then render a new possibility,
something to soften and brighten the otherwise darkly painted world
The hue she sees reveals for her lines of some acceptable clarity
slightly pushing through the clouds to shade a softer, warmer world
Her color gives her now a glimmer of light to create a more cheerful
colored ribbon tied loosely and flowing in the light blue skies in the sky
One that lies just over the crest of the horizon and rekindles the path
that opens widely before her as it's nearing its end that's nearing its end
This is where her new day waits for her again to gently embrace and melt
away the spoils and to keep her feeling free to dream her reality into
sheer existence and shape the world that only *she* truly sees

What If

Everything negative and damaging thought to be
were just a figment of your own deceptive reverie
If worries weren't real and fears never dared to appear
There would be no reason to hold hands with anxiety
or walk worriedly along the edges of the unknown
No strong force could rise up and smash your dreams
like a violent storm whose unexpected winds appear from
nowhere and send you suddenly crashing fast and slamming
you hard against the far reaching distant shore
What would happen if good karma could quickly right any wrong
and the dry seasons of yesterday were now suddenly simply gone
in an instant, without any time to think, and before you noticed
what was to have been your inevitable fate
Imagine sorrow erased from the bank of memory
without evidence of even a single trace
that it had ever existed before
If the bad that caused harm never took seed
the need would change and simply be
a longing for more of the kind of life we'd like to see ... What if?

Simply Complex

Personality plus
Dressed to impress
more or maybe less
So merrily he goes around
mysteriously making his way
through the crowd
working the room
and releasing his energy
determined to spark
interest and excitement
So merrily he makes his usual rounds
eventually unfolding all the facets
of who he is on every side
of what he wants us to see
a revelation of some revolution
that unravels the mysteries that lie within
Somewhere, over there he stands entangled
in his own thoughts and feelings
always yearning to air and share
his inner thoughts and deepest feelings
A nice wrapper on the surface
neatly embodied in sheer simplicity
yet beneath he's clothed in some duplicity
that won't be so easily detected and may go unseen
because there are hidden layers of some obscurity
So there he makes his way, never wanting to be connected to
anyone or held in any one place for too long
Thus, always ready to re-create himself and leaving a question to ponder
which appears at the front of the mind when he exits the room
then lingers behind as some thoughtful food for consideration
Is what you see what you'll *really* get?

2° Below

There is a degree of love that lies below the
measured meter
It can only be manifested to the eye through
a microscopic lens
The existence of a single, solitary emotion
yearning to grow more intense,
if it were only noticed...yet, it's not
And like a butterfly it can't be easily seized
as if it is almost too elusive to be caught
So it remains undetected and unclaimed
eventually condensing itself to nothing
no evidence of even a trace that it ever existed

Let Silence Ring

Let silence bellow from the depths of the soul
as it positions itself to stand so strong, so bold
and shout loudly from all the corners
of those restless racing thoughts
forcing a timeless tranquility to descend
seeking to keep pace with the fine particles
of some momentary perfect stillness it brings
knowing that it will form a force so incredibly strong
that it will eventually permit itself to speak
but only in quiet whispers
It will shatter the noise of sonorous and booming sounds
by clashing with and reverberating against
the walls of elusive peace
Silence threatens to race and roar and reign
and eventually win by calmly staking its claim
Breaking the chains that held peace in abeyance so long
a perfect match has been finally met with this inaudible song
Quietness so robust that tranquility steps in and settles down
at last, to occupy a distantly remote and sacred place for now
A silence that's entrenched in the wanting soul
that wanted to seek soundless solitary time before
but couldn't find a way through those open existing doors
Now, it's solidly set intact, settled comfortably in its new home
Can it offer a brief and welcomed reprieve, for the eyes that weep,
or rescue the racing heart that hears screams but never sleeps?
A resting place can always be found dwelling in the center of a quiet mind

Nature's Best

The evidence of what in life is certain to be mystically unfolds in the seasons of a tree

Winter's barren trunk dressed in daring cold gives the promise to our souls of what's yet to come; the assurance that in time the certainly of spring will soon arrive and announce itself by making its presence known ushering in a coating to cover the frozen ground ; then slowly expand and stretch like an opened umbrella generously spreading itself so colorfully and wide; a prediction turned true in the presence of our opened watchful eyes

Rendering an awe but only for a brief moment; then turning aside to leave our minds infused with ponderous thoughts about when had summer arrived unseen trees fully dressed in crispy green; nature has again left its expected calling card

That time before is soon forgotten as the vibrant hues of fall always unfailingly appear as trees warmly change the landscaping of it all; at last the relief we knew to expect has finally arrived

The chilly precursor will undoubtedly start hanging around before the autumn shed waiting to take its place on center stage once again; a foliage loss will surely follow in due time

There are many mysteries in life not meant to be foreseen but some certainties are always revealed by observing the seasons of a tree

THE PATH UNPAVED

The drum I plainly hear from so many miles afar
pounds loudly in my ear to seek and follow my own star
Though slightly off beat, I answer the call to go to try and find
what lies out there and waits to pair with my still and open mind

Pausing, I yield to an inclination to walk diagonally astray
I choose not to follow the same straight path that's been so clearly paved
It's tried and tested, often strode by the masses, to go that familiar way
The direction from which the sound will come, undoubtedly is still unknown
does it lie in the conventional road for the sake of itself
predestined by design to be taken alone
The straightway that's followed seldom speaks or calls out to me

I must yield instead to that echoing unsteady sound resonating in my heart
though the steps may be far from home and often lead me to a false start
A steady flurry of uneven beats, continue to send a signal to my feet
to follow the jagged path that may sometimes lead me miles away
There is where I'll find my soul in that unnamed place, I pray

Made in the USA
Charleston, SC
26 February 2017